U

Colours

Blue

Gabrielle Woolfitt

Wayland

COLOURS

Blue
Green
Red
Yellow

First published in 1991 by
Wayland (Publishers) Limited
61 Western Road, Hove
East Sussex BN3 1JD, England

Editor: Cath Senker
Designer: Loraine Hayes

Consultant: Tom Collins. Deputy
Headmaster of St Leonards CEP School,
East Sussex

British Library Cataloguing in Publication
Data
Woolfitt, Gabrielle
Blue. – (Colours)
1. Title   II. Series
372.3

ISBN 0-7502-0188-6

Typeset by Kalligraphic Design Ltd,
Horley, Surrey
Printed by G. Canale & C.S.p.A., Turin, Italy
Bound by Casterman S.A., Belgium

Words printed in **bold** are explained in the glossary.

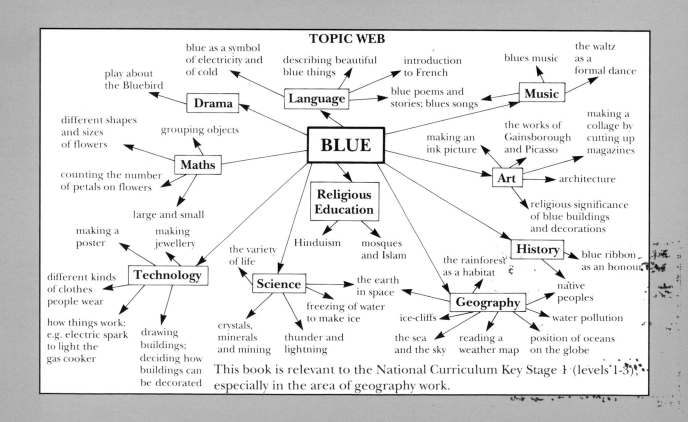

TOPIC WEB

This book is relevant to the National Curriculum Key Stage 1 (levels 1-3), especially in the area of geography work.

CONTENTS

WHAT IS BLUE?

Blue is a natural colour. The sea sometimes looks blue, and so does the sky.

Blue is a musical colour. *The Blue Danube* is a waltz about a river. A waltz is a kind of dance. Sad songs are called blues.

Blue is also an everyday colour. We wear blue jeans. We write with blue pens.

Do you think blue is a beautiful colour? Make a list of beautiful blue things.

FEELING BLUE

This group is singing the blues. Blues songs are about people's **troubles**. What makes you feel blue?

How can you cheer yourself up? You could tell someone why you're blue, or try singing a blues song about your troubles.

Trouble in mind, I'm blue
But I won't be blue always
'Cause the sun gonna shine
In my back door some day

Trouble in mind, yeah yeah I'm blue
But I won't be blue always
Think the wind's gonna change
Blow my blues away.

ELECTRIC
BLUE

Electric sparks can look blue in the dark.

Lightning is a very large electric spark. Lightning is a powerful flash of light, that sometimes looks blue. It is usually followed by thunder. Are you scared of lightning?

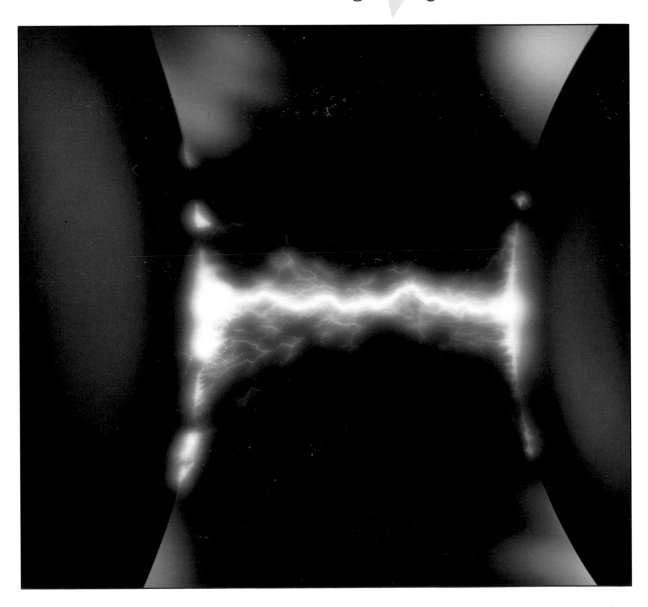

At the fairground, electricity from the roof makes the dodgem cars move. At home, we can use a blue spark to light the gas cooker. Where else have you seen blue sparks? Remember, electricity is dangerous – so don't get too close!

The electricity travels down the poles.

I C E
BLUE

Ice is frozen water. It is made up of **crystals**. Water is **transparent**. So why isn't ice also transparent?

The crystals are broken inside. This makes ice blue.

When white people are cold, they go pink. If a mountain climber gets very cold, her fingers and toes go blue. This is called frostbite. She goes blue with cold.

Where do you see blue as a **symbol** for cold? Find out about the blue symbols on a weather map that mean 'cold'.

BLUE
ANIMALS

These blue parrots live in the **rainforest**. They eat nuts.

What is the kingfisher doing? What does it eat?

The largest animal in the sea is the blue whale. It lives in the sea, but it is not a fish. It is a mammal.

The mother whale feeds the baby whale with her milk. All animals that do this are called mammals.

People hunt whales for their meat and oil. Unless they stop, there will be no whales left in the oceans.

Think of some more blue animals. Are they smaller than the kingfisher? Can they fly? Can they swim?

BLUE
FLOWERS

How many kinds of blue flowers can you see here? Are they all the same shade of blue?

Which flower is the largest? Which has the most petals? Find two flowers with pointed petals. Which has four petals?

speedwell

pale dog violet

scabious

spring squill

crane's-bill

Can you find three flowers with five petals and one with six? Which plant has lots of little flowers on the same stem?

periwinkle

Cut out pictures of blue flowers from a gardening magazine. Stick them on a large sheet of paper to make a poster.

chicory

BLUE
CLOTHES

All sorts of people wear blue clothes. Babies often wear pale blue stretch suits – this colour is called baby blue.

This British policeman wears a dark blue uniform. The people on the right work in blue overalls.

Blue clothes can be beautiful. Do you have any blue clothes? Are they for school, for play or to look smart? Make a chart to show what kind of blue clothes your friends have.

Jeans and dungarees are made from denim.
Denim is a strong material. It is usually blue. Denim is
easy to wash and fun to wear.

BLUE PAINTING

Some artists like to use blue paint. For several years, a famous artist called Picasso only painted blue pictures.

This is *The Blue Boy*. It was painted by an artist called Gainsborough, many years ago.

Blue tiles are used to decorate beautiful **mosques**. Find out about the Blue Mosque in Turkey.

This city is Jodhpur in India. All the blue houses belong to Brahmin priests. They are holy people in the Hindu religion.

Draw and paint a house, or another building. What things in the house could you paint blue?

19

BLUE
WATER

Tap water is **colourless**. So is rain. But look at the water in this picture! Why does the sea sometimes look blue?

Clean water is a good **reflector**, like a mirror. When the sky is blue, the sea looks blue. The water reflects the colour of the sky.

If the water in the sea or a river looks green or brown, it is dirty. It does not reflect the colour of the sky. Dirty water is not a good reflector.

Look at this dirty pond!

Why does the water in a swimming pool look blue?
What colour does the sea look on a cloudy day?
What colour is a lake at night?

BLUE
STORIES

Do you know the story of Bluebeard? Bluebeard was an evil man. He married lots of women. Then he **murdered** them. What happened in the end?

The Bluebird is a play about some children who look for a bluebird. They are helped by a fairy. Their cat and their dog can talk. So can fire and water.

Do you know any poems or songs about blue things? Write your own poem about blue. You could start like this:

Blue is the colour of a
     cloudless sky,
Blue is the colour of the
     sea when it's clean.
When I'm sad I feel blue...

BLUE

IN SPACE

Look at the sky at night. What can you see?
  We do not often see a blue moon! It is very unusual.

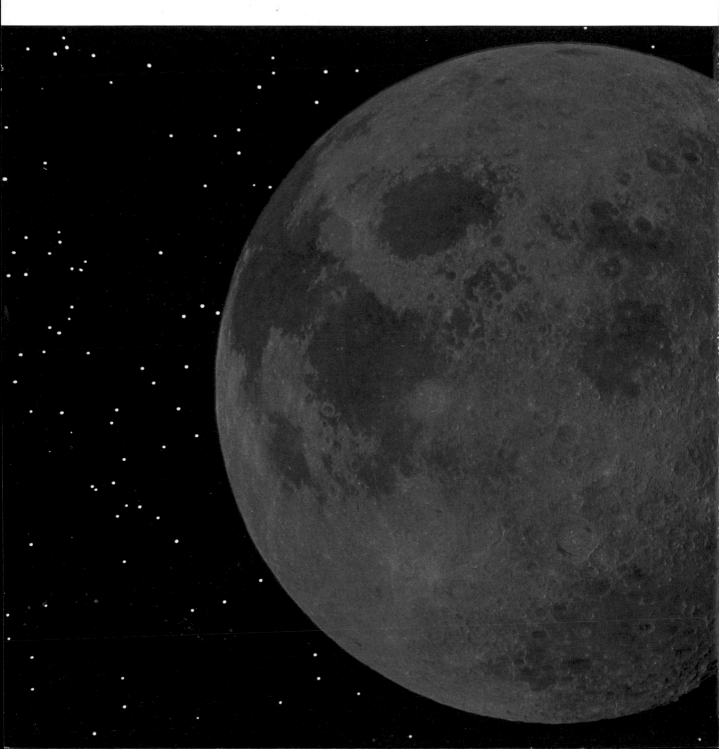

It is caused by dust in the earth's **atmosphere**. If something happens 'once in a blue moon', it hardly ever happens.

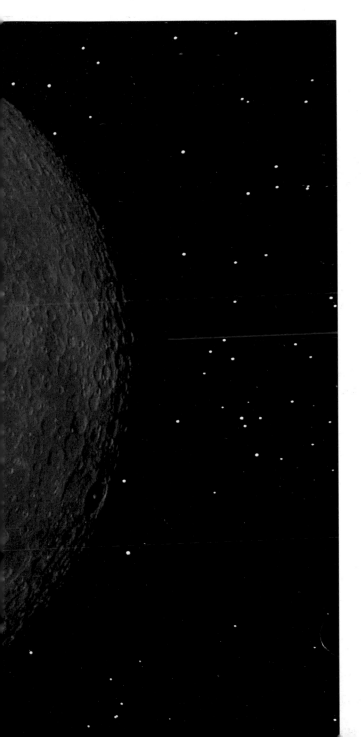

If you are in a spaceship, the earth looks like a big blue ball. Most of the earth is covered by water. Can you see the countries on the **globe**? The seas are shown in blue.

BLUE JEWELS

Some rocks are a beautiful blue colour. People cut out pieces of the rock to make jewels. The jewels are cut into shapes and polished. They are put on rings. What other kinds of jewellery do people wear?

This is a sapphire ring.

Find out about other kinds of jewellery. Which jewels are quite cheap to buy, and which are very expensive?

These **Zuni** women are wearing turquoise jewellery. Turquoise is a greeny-blue stone. The jewellery is made by **native Americans**. They set the jewels in silver.

BLUE
RIBBON

A blue ribbon is sometimes given as a prize. If you are the best, you win the blue ribbon.

The Blue Riband of the Atlantic is a prize for ships. It is given to the **liner** that crosses the **Atlantic Ocean** the fastest.

Cordon bleu means 'blue ribbon' in French. If something is cordon bleu it is very good. Look at this delicious cordon bleu food! Look in a recipe book for a tasty meal you would like to eat.

PROJECT

Ink art

Wear an overall for this!

1. Put some old newspapers on the table.
2. Fold a big sheet of paper in half, and then open it out flat again.
3. Drop some blue ink on one side of the paper with a paintbrush.
4. Draw a pattern in ink.
5. Fold the paper in half and press down.
6. Open the picture. Let it dry.
7. You could use your picture as the cover for a topic book on blue.

GLOSSARY

Atlantic Ocean The second biggest ocean in the world.

Atmosphere The air that is around the earth.

Colourless Without any colour at all.

Crystals Solid, regular shapes, like sugar and salt.

Globe A round ball-shaped map of the earth.

Liner A large ship that carries people.

Mosque A building where Muslims pray.

Murdered Killed on purpose.

Native Americans The people already living in North America when the Europeans started to settle there.

Rainforest A thick forest in a hot place where it rains a lot.

Reflector Something that throws back light, like a mirror.

Symbol Something that stands for or means something else.

Transparent See-through.

Troubles Things that worry you.

Zuni A native American people.

BOOKS TO READ

Into Science: Colour by Terry Jennings (Oxford University Press, 1989)
Let's Look at Outer Space by Jacqueline Dineen (Wayland, 1988)
Let's Look at Rain by Jacqueline Dineen (Wayland, 1988)
Rocks by Terry Jennings (A&C Black, 1990)
Talk about Light by A. Webb and C. Fairclough (Franklin Watts, 1987)
Talk about Water by A. Webb and C. Fairclough (Franklin Watts, 1986)

INDEX

Numbers in **bold** refer to illustrations.

ACKNOWLEDGEMENTS

The photographs in this book were provided by: Bridgeman Art Library 18; Cephas 9
(L. Smith); Chapel Studios 19 (Zul Mukhida); Bruce Coleman 13; Eye Ubiquitous 20
(D. Redfearn); Hutchison 10 (P. Goycolea), 25 (N. Durrell); Photri 6, 27 (J. McCauley); Science
Photo Library 8 (P. Jude); Tony Stone Worldwide COVER, 29; Topham 21 (bottom), 28
(S. Lindblom); Wayland Picture Library 1 and 30 (Zul Mukhida), 16 (left), 17, 21 (top); Zefa 5, 7,
11, 12 (both), 16 (right), 24, 26. Artwork: Jenny Hughes 2, 4–5; Peter Lubach 22–3; John Yates
14–15.